D1068437

ST. THOMAS AND THE
GREEK MORALISTS

Aquinas Lecture 1947, Spring

ST. THOMAS
AND THE
GREEK MORALISTS

Under the Auspices of the Aristotelian Society
of Marquette University

BY

VERNON J. BOURKE, Ph.D.

MARQUETTE UNIVERSITY PRESS
MILWAUKEE 3, WIS.
1947

Nihil Obstat

> Gerard Smith, S.J., censor deputatus
> Milwaukiae, die 5 mensis Januarii, 1948

Imprimatur

> ✠ Moyses E. Kiley
> Archiepiscopus Milwaukiensis
> Milwaukiae, die 5 mensis Januarii, 1948

PREFACE

The Aristotelian Society of Marquette University each year invites a scholar to deliver a lecture in honor of St Thomas Aquinas. Customarily delivered on the Sunday nearest March 7th, the feast day of the Society's patron saint, these lectures are called the Aquinas Lectures.

In 1947 the Society had the pleasure of recording the lecture of Vernon J. Bourke, Ph.D. It was delivered in the Marquette University High School Auditorium Sunday afternoon, March 9.

Vernon J. Bourke was born at North Bay, Ontario, in 1907. He attended St. Michael's College in Toronto, winning the Cardinal Mercier and the Governor General's medals in the philosophy honors course and receiving his B.A. in 1928. He then entered the School of Graduate Studies at the University of Toronto, and was one of the first to attend the Pontifical Institute of Mediaeval Studies where he worked under Etienne Gilson. He gained his M.A. in 1929 and his Ph.D. in 1937.

From 1928 to 1931 Prof. Bourke was lecturer in ancient philosophy at St. Michael's College. In 1931 he joined the faculty of St. Louis University as instructor in philosophy. He was made assistant professor of philosophy in 1938 and associate professor in 1942. In 1946 he became full professor.

He is a past president of the American Catholic Philosophical association, president of the Pontifical Institute of Mediaeval Studies Alumni association and a member of the American Philosophical association, the Mediaeval Academy of America and the Catholic Commission on Intellectual and Cultural Affairs.

Prof. Bourke is also an associate editor of *The Modern Schoolman* and an editorial consultant for the first American printing of the *Opera Omnia* of St. Thomas Aquinas (N.Y., Musurgia, 1948, 25 vols.) He was contributing editor of *Philosophic Abstracts* (Philosophical Library, N.Y.) 1940-45; the *Dictionary of*

Philosophy, 1942 and the *Encyclopedia of Religion,* 1945.

Besides contributing to scholarly journals in this country and Europe, among them *Thought, Speculum, New Scholasticism, Rivista di Filosofia Neoscolastica, St. Louis University Studies,* and *Proceedings of the American Catholic Philosophical association,* he has published four books:

Habitus as a Perfectant of Potency in the Philosophy of St. Thomas Aquinas, doctoral dissertation, School of Graduate Studies, University of Toronto, 1937.

Thomistic Bibliography 1920-1940, Supplement to volume XXI of *The Modern Schoolman,* St. Louis, 1945.

Augustine's Quest of Wisdom, Bruce, Milwaukee, 1945.

Syllabus in Ethical Theory, St. Louis University, 1947.

Another book, on ethics, is being prepared for publication in the Christian Wisdom Series, Macmillan, N.Y.

To these the Aristotelian Society takes pleasure in adding *St. Thomas and the Greek Moralists.*

St. Thomas and the Greek Moralists

S T. THOMAS was not only a great speculative thinker, his was an equally great practical mind. Thomistic moral science owes a great deal to the practical wisdom of the classic Greek moralists. It goes without saying, of course, that the leading Christian theologian of the thirteenth century is much more than an *Aristotelis redivivus*. The world-view of Christian morality has wider horizons than Greek ethics. The New Testament and the Fathers of the Church opened up vistas of human freedom, of supernatural life and action, of comradeship with the angels and even with God, of moral forces such as habitual grace, of the actual fallen condition of mankind, and of an ordination to the ineffable experience of the Beatific Vision, which no pre-Christian Greek saw even dimly. With this rich heritage of Christian spirituality in his background, St. Thomas Aquinas could never revert to the simple naturalism of classic ethics. Yet, the honest scholar cannot read the text of St. Thomas without some due acknowledgment of the positive influence of some Greek ethical teachings on Thomistic thought.

If, in what follows, the major emphasis falls on the historical continuity between certain elements in pagan morality and similar elements in Thomistic morality, and if less stress is placed on the specifically Christian orientation of the practical thought of St. Thomas, let us confess now that Thomas Aquinas was, in all his thinking, a devotee of the religious life, a believing theologian, a follower of Christ, a saint.

St. Thomas as a Moralist

In the past few centuries, it has been the unfortunate custom of many Catholic teachers and writers on moral questions to concede the authority of St. Thomas Aquinas in theoretical philosophy and in speculative theology, but to belittle his power as a moral theologian. The impression is still widespread that the student of moral matters would do well to seek some other guide than St. Thomas.[1] This contention has at least the virtue of forcing us to examine the actual character of St. Thomas' moral thought.

The first thing to be remembered is that St. Thomas nearly always taught as a theologian. In moral philosophy, it is true that we have from him a long and thorough exposition of the *Nicomachean Ethics* of Aristotle.[2] This does not constitute, however, a course in Thomistic ethics. It is an explanation by St. Thomas of what is good and what is faulty in the ethical position of Aristotle. There is not much doubt that this commentary is a contribution to the task of evaluating Aristotelian philosophy—a task which was imposed on the professors of the University of Paris when, rather suddenly, they came into the possession of the Latin versions of the major works of Aristotle.[3] It became a matter of concern to the ecclesiastical authorities, when, not only professors of liberal arts but also professors of theology began avidly to read and teach the new-found science and philosophy of Aristotle. From the year 1210 onward, several Councils forbade the teaching, either in public or private, of the works of Aristotle on natural philosophy.[4] Yet the personal reading of Aristotle was not expressly forbidden. The wording, "non legantur," obviously refers to the use of Aristotle in public or private lectures. But the problem remained: what to do with this vast encyclopedia of pagan learning? It was suspected that Aristotle had some anti-Catholic teachings, yet there was no official tendency to throw away the wheat with the chaff.

In the year 1231, Pope Gregory wrote with obvious care, but in no spirit of obscurantism: "these books of natural science which have been prohibited for a definite reason by a provincial Council may not be used at Paris, until they have been examined and all suspicion of error removed."[5] To carry out this task of investigation and correction, the Pope named a commission of three scholars. Information is lacking as to what they did, but it appears that they never finished the work.

There is no evidence that the parts of the *Nicomachean Ethics* available at this time were ever regarded with much suspicion. Theological works of the decade 1225-1235 contain rather frequent reference to the *Ethics*.[6] St. Albert the Great refers about forty times to Aristotle, in his earliest treatise on practical morality, the *Tractatus de natura boni.* This work is thought to date from the years 1236-1237.[7] However, it was probably about mid-century that St. Albert did his *Commentary on the Ethics,* using a method of paraphrase suggested by the works of Avicenna. The style of the commentaries by St. Thomas, on the other hand, is more akin to that of Averroës. After a methodical analysis of each phrase of the Aristotelian text, he expounded the views of Aristotle rather objectively, only criticizing where there was manifest opposition between the Greek philosopher and Christian doctrine. One product of this enterprise was the *Exposition of the Nicomachean Ethics*. One may readily see that, important though it may be, this commentary is not St. Thomas' exposition of his own science of morals.

It is necessary, then, to turn to the other works of St. Thomas to find his developed theory of morality. In addition to certain *opuscula,* these works are the *Lectures on the Second and Third Books of Sentences* (1254-1256); the *Quaestiones Disputatae de Veritate* (1256-1259); certain of the *Quaestiones Quodlibetales* (from 1256 on); the *Summa contra Gentiles (chiefly Book III,* 1259-1261); the *Summa Theologica* (chiefly I-II, and II-II, 1266-1272); the *Quaestiones Disputatae de Malo* (1268-1269); the *Quaestiones Disputatae de Virtutibus* (1269-1272); and the *Compendium Theologiae* (1271-1273). This means that, when we treat St. Thomas as a moralist, it is not as a natural ethician but as a moral theologian that he is to be considered primarily; for, these are all theological works. It also serves to remind us that there is no one treatise of Thomistic morality, which might be used as a textbook in the teaching of ethics.

The *Prima Secundae* is the most finished treatise on general moral theory, as the *Secunda Secundae* is for special moral questions. Both require to be supplemented by reference to the other works, because the *Summa Theologica* is frequently terse and economical of words, where the *Quaestiones Disputatae* are more ample in their explanations. This marks a second characteristic of St. Thomas the moralist: his open-mindedness. Histories of philosophy often refer to him as a synthetic thinker, a man who systematized Christian learning in the thirteenth century. If this suggests that he erected a closed system with answers to all the problems of Christian morality, then it is not true. St. Thomas realized full well the difficulty and complexity of practical reasoning. He approached these problems many times; sometimes changing his point of view. He never claimed to have written the last word on any problem.

To the philosopher, the most striking quality of the moral science of St. Thomas is its firm foundation in metaphysics. This is quite apparent in the development of thought in the *Summa Theologica*. The *First Part* makes full use of his theory of being, in the explanation of the existence and attributes of God, in the study of Creation as a divine Act and as a product, finally in the acute analysis of the nature and potencies of man. This metaphysics of human nature continues without break into the *Prima Secundae*; until, after the treatise on the end of man and the nature of the voluntary act, one finds that the thought has become more and more oriented to the problems of morality. As a consequence, it is most difficult to determine the starting point of the moral teaching of the *Summa Theologica*. The progress of thought is continuous and homogeneous. Speculative theology and metaphysics grow into moral theology. The philosophical base of the ethical theory of St. Thomas is metaphysics. It is a bad error in method to read the definitely moral sections of the *Pars Secunda* without a good understanding of the metaphysics of the *Pars Prima.* This metaphysical groundwork distinguishes the morality of St. Thomas from much recent writing on Catholic morality. From the fourteenth century onward, law (either canon or civil) became the basis of most moral works. St. Thomas was not unaware of the importance of canon law; he was strongly influenced by it, particularly in the choice of particular examples or moral cases.[8] But the "legalism" of the later Scholastic moral theologians (remember that both F. Suarez and St. Alphonsus Liguori were trained in law before entering upon the study of theology) is foreign to Thomistic moral science.

The Greek Moralists

A preliminary words is necessary, too, in explanation of the phrase, Greek moralists. One of the historical problems in the study of Thomism is the relative influence of the

views of the *Sancti* and the *Philosophi,* in the
background of any special question. A former
Aquinas lecturer (the late E. K. Rand) has ex-
pressed some polite amazement at the extensive
references to Cicero, in the *Summa Theologica.*
The fact is that St. Thomas habitually orna-
mented his texts with citations from more
than two hundred authors. It does not take
the intelligent reader long to see that, on
philosophical points at least, these *auctoritates*
are not given for the sake of advancing the
argument. Aquinas relies very little on the
argument from authority. His rich documen-
tation is there to show the relation of his
thought to various traditions, to clarify his
terminology for the student, to situate his
views historically, to appraise and criticize
his predecessors—but, it is human experience
and demonstrative reasoning which form the
warp and woof of his argument.[9]

In this array of historical references, which
are remarkably accurate considering the condition of the texts available in the thirteenth
century, the Greek philosophers of the classic

and Hellenistic periods are quite prominent.
The Pre-Socratics, Socrates, Plato and Aristotle,
Zeno the Stoic, Chrysippus, Epicurus, Philo
Judaeus, Andronicus, Plotinus, Proclus, Por-
phyry, Simplicius and Themistius—these are
the leading names. St. Thomas did not know
their writings in the original Greek.[10] He read
translations, when he had them, but many
of the Greek authors were only known at
second hand, through fragments and para-
phrases in the Roman and Patristic writers in
Latin. This need occasion no surprise, for
even with modern advances in classical schol-
arship, we are still very dependent on Latin
sources for our knowledge of Greek Stoicism
and Epicureanism.

It will not be possible to take each Greek
moral writer and investigate his possible influence on St. Thomas. Let us concentrate, instead, on the examination of two major
schools of Greek moral philosophy: Aristotelianism and Stoicism. We will try to show
that St. Thomas received at least some positive inspiration from these sources.

The philosophy of Aristotle is an important element in the Greek background of Thomistic morality. This is not simply a question of the influence of the *Nicomachean Ethics,* but of the whole *corpus* of Aristotle. The moral conclusions of St. Thomas would probably have been much the same had he not known Aristotle. The historical fact remains, however, that the physics, metaphysics, philosophy of the soul, and the ethics of Aristotle strongly affected the way in which St. Thomas arrived at his practical conclusions. It is not that St. Thomas simply re-wrote, or even re-thought, Aristotle.[11] More and more, mediaeval scholars are coming to realize the complexity and richness of the historical sources of Thomism, and the consequent inadequacy of the older view that St. Thomas merely "baptized" Aristotle. Nonetheless, we must not go to the opposite extreme of underestimating the Aristotelian content of Thomistic wisdom.

Stoicism, on the other hand, exerted a partial but continuous influence in almost every century of Christian moral thinking. With Epicureanism, it was the dominant practical philosophy of the pagans throughout the early centuries of the Catholic Church. The Fathers were much more favorable to Stoicism than to Epicureanism. The first great moral treatise in the Latin Church, is the *De Officiis Ministrorum* written in the fourth century by St. Ambrose.[12] It is not too much to say that no mediaeval work on morality is without some debt to this pioneer treatise of the Bishop of Milan. Thoroughly Christian in its spirit, this *De Officiis* is constantly modelled on the work, with almost the same name, by Cicero. And the *De Officiis* of Cicero is, in turn, patterned on the Greek treatise, περὶ καθήκοντος, of the Stoic Panaetius. What we have, here, is a sequence of three moral studies, from the second century before Christ to the fourth century after Christ, in which the underlying philosophic position is Stoicism.[13] Since St. Augustine of Hippo is undoubtedly the greatest Patristic authority in the Western Church, and since the ethical position of Augustine is much dependent on that of Ambrose (with direct reinforcement from Augustine's own reading of Cicero and Varro), the weight of moral conviction in the early Church is, in good part, Stoic. This is not to deny the presence of Platonism in the thought of the Fathers. But, *in moral questions,* the first great Greek influence is definitely that of Stoicism. We shall try to see how some of this carries over into Thomism.

There are other philosophical elements in the pre-history of St. Thomas' moral thought. Platonism, Epicureanism, Neo-platonism and Scepticism are of some importance. With the exception of certain aspects of Neo-platonism, these are chiefly negative influences. Aristotelianism and Stoicism are more positive. To demonstrate this, we may consider three key topics in the practical thought of St. Thomas: (1) the structure of the moral act; (2) right reason as the rule of morality; and (3) the organization of moral problems under the virtues.

The Structure of the Moral Act

In his study of the voluntary act, found only in the *Summa Theologica* as a fully developed theory, St. Thomas presents a truly remarkable analysis of the psychological factors of morality.[14] Man is described as using intellect and will in a progressive duality of functions, working to the completion of the moral action. The first four steps have to do with the end of the act: (1) the intellect apprehends the end and presents it to the will; (2) the will wishes *(velle)* this end; (3) the intellect judges that the end is to be sought by the agent; (4) the will then intends *(intendere)* this end. The next four steps are concerned with the means to this end: (5) the intellect deliberates, or takes counsel *(consilium)* concerning the various possible means; (6) the will consents *(consensus)* to the previous judgment, which may simply mean an approval of several possible means; (7) the intellect judges that one means is preferable and should be used *(sententia)*; (8) the will

chooses, or elects, the one means to be used
(electio). Finally, there are four steps in the
order of execution: (9) the intellect, in association with will, orders that the means be used
(imperium); (10) the will actively initiates the
use of the means *(usus)*; (11) the intellect apprehends the fittingness of the act being per-
formed; and (12) the will rejoices in the performance of a good work *(fruitio)*. The last
two steps take the agent back to the end, for
they involve the relation of the commanded
act to this end. It is to be remembered that we
are speaking analytically, when we say that
the intellect acts, or the will acts; it is really
the substantial moral agent who is acting,
through intellect or will.

Now, what is the source of this analysis?
One modern scholar has maintained that there
is nothing like it in the thirteenth century, that
it must be completely an invention of the
genius of St. Thomas.[15] But there is a background for this theory of the structure of the
human act.

Let us read a passage from the *De Fide Orthodoxa* of St. John Damascene; the English is from the Latin version of Burgundio of Pisa, which was probably what St. Thomas read, but we have collated this with the Greek text in order to show the sequence of the original psychological terms.[16]

St. John writes:

We should know that our soul has two kinds of powers (*virtutes*): one kind is cognitive, the other vital (*zotica, τὸ ξωτικόν*). Intellect, mind (*mens*), opinion, imagination and sense are cognitive; counsel (*consilium, βούλησις*) and election (*electio, προαίρεσις*) are vital, or appetitive . . . [There follows an explanation of two forms of appetition: *θέλησις* and *βούλησις*. Burgundio's version is wordy and none too clear at this point, but the distinction in the original follows these lines: the natural tendency to be, and to live, and to move vitally, is called *θέλησις*, when

this tendency is found in rational
beings. So, Burgundio translates θέλησις,
as *voluntas*. On the other hand, βούλησις
is the initial *movement* of rational ap-
petite, i.e. of θέλησις, towards a definite end.]

Thus, [continues St. John Damas-
cene] βούλησις, that is *voluntas,* is for
the end, and not for the means to the
end. Therefore, the end is what is wished
(βουλητόν), for instance: to be a king,
or to be healthy. But the means to the
end is that concerning which counsel is
taken *(consiliabile,* βουλευτόν) that is,
the way in which we ought to be
healthy, or to rule.

Then, after counsel and the will-act
[Burgundio writes *bulisim*], come search
(inquisitio, ζήτησις) and examination
(scrutatio, σκέψις); and after these, if
it be concerning things within our
power, comes counsel *(consilium,*
βουλή), that is, counselling *(consiliatio,*
βούλευσις) for counsel is a searching

appetition *(appetitus inquisitivus)* for those things which are within our power; one takes counsel as to whether one ought to carry out a task, or not. Next, one judges what is better, and this is called judgment *(judicium, κρίσις)*. Next, one is disposed [here, Burgundio renders διατίθεται by the active, *disponit,* thereby causing confusion in the mind of the mediaeval reader] and loves what has been judged in counselling, and this is called preference *(sententia, γνώμη)*; for, if one judged and were not disposed toward the result of this judgment, that is, if one did not like it, that would not be called preference *(sententia)*. Then after disposition (διάθεσις), comes election προαίρεσις); now election is to choose one rather than the other from the two preceding possibilities. Next, one makes a movement toward action, and this is called impulse *(impetus, ὁρμή)*. Next, one carries out the action, and this is called use *(usus, χρῆσις)*. Finally, one desists from appetition, after the use *(παύεται)*.

The indebtedness of St. Thomas to this text of John Damascene is obvious. It contains many of the elements of the structural analysis of the human act, as found in the *Prima Secundae*. The Greek Father has taken over and developed certain suggestions from the psychology and the ethics of Aristotle.[17] In the discussion of the act of choice, Aristotle remarks that it is like an appetitive act of intellection, or an intellective act of appetition.[18] St. John Damascene has opened up the Aristotelian discussion by taking the question of the moral decision as a step-by-step process, working from the consideration of the end, through the means, to the performance of the commanded act. Some elements in St. Thomas' treatment are terminologically related to traditional Augustianism. This is true of *intentio, usus* and *frui*.[19] St. Thomas acknowledges John Damascene as his source by constant references throughout questions eight to seventeen of the *Secunda Secundae.* At times, he quotes Nemesius' psychological definitions, and here again he is using an author whose philosophy of man is fundamentally Aristotelian.[20]

Briefly, St. Thomas' psychological analysis of the moral act is an outgrowth of Aristotle's speculation, transmitted through the Greek Fathers, enlarged by some borrowings from St. Augustine. One might say that the structure of the analysis is suggested by Damascene, the psychological principles by Aristotle, some of the Latin terms (and the strong emphasis on the will-acts) by Augustine. The final formulation in the *Prima Secundae* is the product of St. Thomas' own genius, but not without aid from his predecessors.[21] The moral psychology of St. Thomas is a development of Aristotle's philosophy of the soul.

Right Reason as the Rule of Morality

A second striking feature of the moral view of St. Thomas is his emphasis on reason.

This is not an anti-religious, naturalistic rationalism, but a firm conviction that all beings exist, and do, or should, operate according to the law of reason. As the reader of the *Prima Secundae* is frequently reminded: "The rule and measure of human acts is reason, which is the first principle of human acts."[22]

The good moral act is in conformity with right reason *(recta ratio)*. All acts of all the moral virtues must stem from prudence, which is *recta ratio agibilium*.[23] While the human will is the dynamic faculty, efficiently producing the moral act, St. Thomas regards the reasoning intellect as the formal principle of the moral quality of the act. "Ille actus quo voluntas tendit in aliquid quod proponitur ut bonum, ex eo quod per rationem est ordinatum ad finem, materialiter quidem est voluntatis, formaliter autem rationis."[24]

What, precisely, is this right reason which is the rule of human morality? An important controversy, centering on this question, has gone on in the past three decades. One group of interpreters, influenced by the ethics of

Suarez, reduces right reason to the conformity
of human acts with the nature of man, adequately considered in all its essential moral
relations.[25] There are other Thomistic scholars who maintain that right reason is the
"dictate" of the faculty of reason.[26] St.
Thomas' own position is broader than that
of either school of modern interpretation.

Man is, according to St. Thomas, a member of a definite species, formally character-
ized by the possession of a reasoning intellect.
This is a matter of metaphysics: the perfec-
tion, even in the area of operations, of any
being is to be in act to the fullest extent in
accord with the formal act of its being. The
ratio hominis is at once a principle of the
species man, and a principle of rightness in
human thought and voluntary action.[27] In the
order of the acts of reasoning, terminating in
right judgments, man's intellect does not
work in a vacuum. The speculative reason
judges rightly when it is conformed to the existing nature of its real objects. Practical reasoning, on the other hand, is ruled, or recti-

fied, by the judgments of speculative reason. The rightness, or wrongness, of a practical judgment—and of the resultant moral act—is determined, not by a direct comparison of the proposed act with the natures of things, but by the conformity, or nonconformity, of practical reasoning with speculative reasoning, through which the real order is primarily known. Existing things regulate speculative reason; speculative reason, thus rectified, regulates practical reasoning.[28]

Nor is it merely by finite realities that human reason is regulated and made right. The reason of man is part of the order of Divine Providence. Man is submitted, in actual existence to the rule, from above, of the Divine Mind, the *Ratio Dei.*[29] St. Thomas did not neglect St. Augustine's teaching on the *ratio superior* and the *ratio inferior.*[30] The same human reason may look downward to earthly things, or upward to the eternal reasons of God. To consider the value of a human act from the point of view of its ordination to the ultimate end of man, or in rela-

tion to the Eternal Law, or even to come to an
ultimate moral decision, is, according to St.
Thomas, the function of superior reason.[31]
God is the supreme *Ratio* and He is the Source
of rightness in all other *rationes*.

The moral order is the order of reason;
not the order of *entia rationis*, but of real
beings governed in existence and in operation
by the Reason and Law of God. In this real
order of reason, the human intellect reasons
under the guidance of the *Ratio Dei*, from
above, and in keeping with the reasons or formal principles, of finite beings. Man's reason
is not the cause of the formal specification of
the things of nature. In a sense, man's intellect is subject to these natural things every
time it elicits a speculative judgment about
reality. But man's practical reason is the proximate formal cause of the goodness and rightness of human acts, because these acts are pro-
duced under the dominion of human reason.
Man's relation to his moral acts is something
like that of an artist to his artifacts; their
goodness is measured by their conformity to

the thoughts from which they proceed. But human reason is not the ultimate measure of moral goodness. The primary rule of morality is the *Ratio Dei,* which is identical with the Divine Law. This is why St. Thomas can say: "For the human will, there is a double rule *(regula duplex):* one is proximate and homogeneous [with the will], namely human reason itself; the other is the prime rule, namely the Eternal Law, which is, as it were, the Reason of God."[32]

One may be forgiven the length of this exposition of a fundamental and difficult point, on which the whole moral theory of St. Thomas hinges. The question may now be asked: where did he get this concept of the moral order of reason?

We all know that the early Greeks had a tremendous respect for reason. This is one of the marks of classical culture. It is present in nearly all Greek philosophers. Aristotle is one of its devoted exponents. His lines, in the tenth book of the *Nicomachean Ethics,*[33] come immediately to mind: "for man, therefore, the life according to reason is best and pleasantest, since reason more than anything else *is* man. This life is also the happiest." But Aristotle never thought of the order of moral reason as St. Thomas did. There is completely lacking, in the original Aristotelianism, the ordering of free human acts to an *objectively real,* ultimate end. Aristotle's man looks only to subjective self-perfection; his God has nothing to do with human acts.

The case is quite different with Stoicism. Chrysippus and Zeno taught that man should live in accord with nature. They appear to have differed as to whether nature is that of the individual man, or that of the cosmos.[34] However, they and all their followers are in agreement when they say that to live in accord with nature is to live in conformity with right reason.[35] Cleanthes' *Hymn to Zeus* is an apostrophe of the universal law of reason. Though the Greek Stoics are materialistic, naturalistic and pantheistic in their concept of divinity, at least they conceived of a deity which could be an immutable guide for moral action. It is a case of a low-grade metaphysics accompanied by high-grade moral ideals. Their right reason (ὀρθὸς λόγος) is one of the high points in Greek ethics.

Moreover, St. Thomas could hardly have avoided the influence of this Stoic concept. It came to him through both the traditions of Latin literature in which he was trained. The classical writers of Rome, with their Christian expositors, make up one tradition. Cicero, Seneca, Marcus Aurelius and Macrobius transmit Greek Stoicism to the Middle Ages. They are aided by the grammarians and rhetoricians of the liberal arts tradition, by Boethius, Cassiodorus and Isidore of Seville. Roman political theory, law, and educational theory are founded on the respect for reason. John of Salisbury's *Polycraticus* shows how much of this was retained by the mediaeval scholar. St. Thomas was well trained in this liberal tradition.

The other literature which St. Thomas knew well was that of the Latin Fathers of the

Church. Here, St. Ambrose and St. Augustine are the leading authors. We have seen that Ambrose's *De Officiis* is a conscious adaptation of Cicero to Christian needs.[36] The Fathers kept what was reasonable and good in Stoicism, and they enlarged its view of the law of reason to take in the order of Divine Providence. Even the Stoic ideal, of a life of reason undisturbed by passion, had considerable appeal for the Christian moralist. If the condition of apathy ever meant to the Stoics the complete stilling of all sense feelings, then this is an unnatural virtue for man; but St. Thomas displays good historical insight, when he remarks that this may be understood in a good sense, if it be taken to mean control of *inordinate* passion.[37]

We may have no hesitation in concluding that the *recta ratio* of St. Thomas finds some of its roots in Greek Stoicism. It is quite in keeping with Aristotelianism and Augustinism, but these philosophies do not stress the theory to the extent that Stoicism does.

The Ordering of Moral Problems

Probably every moral writer experiences some difficulty in the effort to arrange and order the manifold problems of human life. It is hard to find a method of treatment which will make room for the many special questions to be discussed, and which will not be too complicated. This was a problem of method, faced by St. Thomas in the treatises on special morality in the *Secunda Secundae*.

Instead of arranging his treatment according to the various types of sins, or with reference to the duties of man to God, to other men, to himself, and in regard to material things (a method used in many moral works before and after the thirteenth century), St. Thomas chose to organize his material under the seven chief virtues. We may read his reasons for this choice, in the prologue to the *Secunda Secundae*:

"After the general consideration of the virtues and vices, and other things pertaining to moral matters, it is neces-

sary to consider singular problems in a
special way. For, universal statements
about moral problems are not very use-
ful, since actions go on in the area of
particulars.

"Now anything connected with
moral matters may be considered in a
special way, from two points of view.
In one way, from the aspect of the
moral matter itself, thus we may think
of this virtue or that vice. In another
way, in relation to the special states of
different men, we may, for instance,
consider those who come under some-
one's authority, and prelates, or the
followers of the active and the contem-
plative life, or whatever other differences there are among men. Therefore,
we shall first of all consider, in a special way, those things which pertain
to the common state of all men; sec-
ondly, in a special way, those things
which pertain to determinate states of
life.

"We should consider, in connection with the first, that if we have determined certain points above [i.e. in general moral theory] concerning virtues, gifts, vices and precepts, a great deal more must be said about them now. For, he who wishes to treat, in an adequate way, the precept: 'Thou shalt not commit adultery,' must study, in regard to adultery, the kind of sin that it is, and how the knowledge of it depends on the knowledge of the virtue to which it is opposed. Therefore, the method of consideration will be more complete and more expeditious, if at the same time and in the same treatise consideration be given to the virtue and its corresponding gift, to the opposed vices, and to the affirmative or negative precepts.

"This method of consideration will be suitable to the vices taken in their proper species, for it has been shown above that vices and sins are specifi-

cally diversified according to their matter or object, and not according to
other distinctions of sins, for instance,
of the heart, of the mouth, and of
deeds, or according to weakness, ignor-
ance, and malice, and other differences
of this kind. It is the same matter in regard to which a virtue operates rightly,
and in regard to which the opposed
vices recede from rectitude.

"When the whole matter of morals
is thus reduced to the consideration of
the virtues, all the virtues are to be reduced further, to seven: three of these
are the theological, which must be
treated first; and the other four are cardinal, and they will be treated after-
wards. One of the intellectual virtues
is prudence, and it is included and
numbered among the cardinal virtues.
But art does not pertain to moral science, which is concerned with things
that can be done, since art is right reason in regard to things which can be

made, as has been said above. And the
other three intellectual virtues, wisdom, understanding and science, have
the same names as some of the Gifts of
the Holy Spirit; hence, consideration
will be given them at the same time
that the Gifts corresponding to the virtues are being considered. The other
moral virtues all reduce in some way to
the cardinal virtues, as appears from
what has been said above; hence, in the
consideration of each cardinal virtue,
all the virtues pertaining in any way to
it, and the opposed vices, will also be
considered. And in this way nothing
will be overlooked in the field of
morals."

This Thomistic method of using the three
theological and the four cardinal virtues as
the principles of organization of special
morality represents a break with the tradition
of pre-Thomistic Christian moralists.[38] St.
Thomas seems to have found the suggestion

for this, in the classic theory of the "parts" of the cardinal virtues.[39] Though this theory goes back at least to Plato,[40] the first important use of it is in the sixth book of the *Nicomachean Ethics*. It became common among the later Greek and Roman ethicians to make long lists of the integral elements of each major virtue, to append definitions of the different species of prudence, justice, temperance and fortitude, to mention subordinate virtues which were like the main ones. The chief authors of these lists of virtues are Aristotle, Andronicus, Cicero, Plotinus, Seneca, and Macrobius.

As a typical instance of this sort of listing of the "parts" of the major virtues, we may consider the treatise *De Affectibus*. This was, apparently, a Latin version of a work by a Greek author named Andronicus.[41] The work opens with an explanation of the four chief passions of the soul, as departures from right reason; this is obviously Stoicism.[42] Then the four virtues are presented as means of controlling the passions. This is followed by general definitions of the four virtues: prudence, temperance, justice and fortitude. These definitions are trite, not original, of no great interest to St. Thomas.

Andronicus proceeds to a particular treatment of each cardinal virtue, and it is here that he lists their associated parts.[43] These lists, with Andronicus' definitions of each part, do interest St. Thomas. He carefully compares the names and definitions of the "parts" given by Andronicus with other classic lists. From these sources, he develops his very thorough analysis of the respective fields, or *matters,* of the four principal virtues. His method is most obvious in the *Commentary on the Sentences,* but it is followed in all his later divisions of the subject matter of morality.

If we look at the beginning of the treatise on each cardinal virtue, in the *Secunda Secundae,* we find St. Thomas again quoting these classic lists of virtues[44] and then making up his own list of parts. It is from this background that the triple classification of integral, subjective and potential parts seems to stem.

Of course, the pagan writers do not figure with any prominence in the handling of the theological virtues. Faith and hope are treated with reference to Biblical and Patristic sources. We have the feeling that St. Thomas is a little sorry that he can find no Greek background for these characteristically Christian virtues. He seems to experience some relief, when he reaches charity.[45] Here, he makes extensive use of Aristotle's long treatise on friendship, from the seventh and eighth books of the *Nicomachean Ethics*.[46]

The point, here, is not that St. Thomas is deriving the main thought of his special morality from the Greeks. He is too Christian in spirit for that. It is a matter of method. The Thomistic ordering of the special questions of morality under the virtues finds its methodological source in the lists of virtues common to most classic writers in the Aristotelian tradition. On this point, Stoicism is not so important, though some of the authors of these lists, in Roman times, are partly of Stoic convictions.

The General Influence of the Greek Moralists

What we have seen constitutes only a sampling of the broad problem of the influence of the Greek Moralists on the thought of St. Thomas. Taking the three points which have been examined in the reverse order, that is, from the third back to the first, we may conclude that, (1) the *material* approach to the questions of moral science is developed by St. Thomas from the analytic study of the four virtues of the classic Greek and Roman ethicians; (2) the *formal* element in Thomistic morality is derived from the Greek reverence for right reason; and (3) the metaphysical analysis of the structure of the moral act stems from Greek ethics, through St. John Damascene.

Had other aspects of Thomistic moral science been chosen, many points would have been found in regard to which the Greeks have not been so influential. This is true, of course, of the important question of the ultimate end of human actions. On this point, St.

Thomas went far beyond the teleology of Aristotle and the cosmic reason of the Stoics.[47] It has become commonplace for readers of St. Thomas to claim that there are two ultimate ends for man, one natural, the other supernatural.[48] As a corollary of this theory of a double ultimate end, we find the supposition that St. Thomas followed the principles of Aristotelian philosophy in treating of the *natural* end and happiness of man,[49] and the revealed truth of Christianity in dealing with the *supernatural* end.

Full comment on this interpretation of St. Thomas' view of the ultimate end of man is not possible here, but one may offer the following suggestions for clarification. First of all, the tendency in the works of Catholic theologians to distinguish radically between two orders of life and action, the natural and the supernatural, becomes marked in the Renaissance period. The distinction is not so sharp in the thought of St. Thomas.[50] It is quite plain that the Angelic Doctor did not confuse supernatural principles of existence and action with natural principles. He knew that the agent intellect is not the *lumen gloriae*. However, St. Thomas also knew that it is one thing to consider speculatively an abstraction which does not exist, for example a man operating morally in a state of pure nature, and that it is quite another thing to reason about the moral problems of man, *as he does exist*. It would be possible to develop a moral theory of the natural man and his natural end. This would be speculation; just as much speculation as to attempt to answer the question: what would have been the present condition of the human race had Adam not sinned? Thomistic moral science does not treat such speculative issues. It is concerned with the actual problems of man trying to perform good voluntary actions under existing conditions. One of these existing conditions is the moral handicap imposed upon the human agent by the loss of original justice. Another such condition is the availability of sanctifying grace. A purely natural ethics ignores, or abstracts from, these real conditions. It attempts to think of man *as if* he were unrelated to supernatural principles and to reason *as if* man had a purely natural, ultimate end. But the moral science of St. Thomas is not an *Als Ob* philosophy. That is why there is only one ultimate end for man, according to this science.[51] This end is God, as seen in the beatific vision.[52]

The Greek moralists did not know this end. Aristotle and the Stoics did not know that man was to enjoy personal immortality; still less did they suspect the possibility of a human participation in divine happiness. Yet they did experience a vague yearning for a supreme God, Who would be an object of perfect contemplation. This teaching was found by St. Thomas in a small treatise known in the thirteenth century as *De Bona Fortuna*. Compiled from moral works, either of Aristotle or of some member of his immediate school,[53] this little book teaches that there is a higher principle, or standard, of morality than human reason. To St. Thomas, it suggested that the best of the Greeks aspired to a contemplation of God.[54] That, among other reasons is why the Aristotelianism of St. Thomas never caused him to detach the natural from the supernatural.

Greek philosophy is one source of Thomistic wisdom. It is not necessary to maintain that it is the sole, or most important, source. St. Thomas used whatever he could find in the works of the Greek moralists, provided it was not opposed to his religious convictions and provided it would help to clarify Christian moral science.[55] But he was fully aware of the inadequacy of Greek ethics, as we may read in one of his last works:[56]

> And this also is clear: not one of the philosophers before the coming of Christ could with all his striving, know as much about God and the things needed for eternal life, as would an old woman, by faith, after the coming of Christ.

NOTES

1. In an interesting discussion of this point, in the *Bulletin Thomiste* IV (1936) pp. 639-645, Father J. M. Ramirez, O.P., reviewing the article, "Probabilisme," *Dictionnaire de Théologie Catholique*, XIII, col. 417-619 (which article by T. Deman, O.P., may also be read with profit in this connection), attributes this shift away from the moral science of Thomism to, "une extension indue et déraisonnable du juridique pur à tout l'ordre moral," (*Bull. Thom.* p. 641, citing Deman, col. 473.) Later, Father Ramirez adds: "Il n'est pas exact de dire que S. Thomas est le théologien du dogme, S. Alphonse celui de la morale; ni même que S. Thomas est le docteur du dogme et de la théologie morale spéculative, S. Alphonse celui de la morale pratique. S. Thomas est le docteur de la morale spéculative et pratique parce que sa morale est essentiellement ordonnée à l'action et contient un système complet de l'acte humain et de ses règles." (p. 642).

    Without venturing any opinion in the field of moral theology, I should like to suggest that this judgment of the importance of Thomistic moral science is certainly true in the philosophic order. The notion that St. Thomas will do as a metaphysician but that it is necessary to go to Suarez, or some other thinker, for ethics, is responsible for the lack of integration in many a philosophical course in modern Catholic colleges.

2. Apart from printings in the *Opera Omnia,* this work is found in only one modern edition which is commercially available: *In decem libros Ethicorum Aristotelis ad Nicomachum Expositio,* cura A. Pirotta, Turin, Marietti, 1934, xxiv—747 pp.

3. Two (Books II-III) and eventually a third (Book I) of the *Nic. Eth.* were in Latin at the end of the 12th century. This was the "Old Ethics." Robert Grosseteste made the first complete Latin version, about 1240-1243 A.D. It was long supposed that St. Thomas used a revision of Grosseteste's translation, made by William of Moerbeke; see, Franceschini, E., "S. Tommasso e l'Etica nicomachea," *Rivista di Filos. neoscolastica* (1936) pp. 313-328. But Father Keeler has shown that the text read by Aquinas was substantially that of Grosseteste, and that there is no real evidence that the revisions, of which there are some, were done for St. Thomas by Moerbeke. Incidentally, the so-called "old Latin version" printed now with the exposition of St. Thomas, is not precisely the text used by St. Thomas. See: L. W. Keeler, S.J., "The Alleged Revision of Robert Grosseteste's Translation of the Ethics," *Gregorianum* XVIII (1937) pp. 410-425, in which the methods of research of Franceschini are bluntly criticized.

The reader may now be referred to the magistral study of M. Grabmann, which was published after the writing of the original draft of this lecture: *Guglielmo di Moerbeke O.P. il traduttore delle opere di Aristotele.* (I papi del Duecento

e l'Aristotelismo II. Roma, Pont. Univ. Gregori-
ana, 1946, XII-194 pp.) The second chapter of
Grabmann's work gives a definitive account of the
original translations and the revisions made by
William of Moerbeke, and of the translator's relations with Pope Gregory X and St. Thomas
Aquinas.

4. The Council of Paris (A.D. 1210), presided
over by Peter of Corbeil, Archbishop of Sens,
ruled: "nec libri Aristotelis de naturali philosophia nec commenta legantur Parisius publice vel
secreto . . ." *Chartularium Universitatis Parisien-
sis* (ed. Denifle et Chatelain, Paris, 1889) I, 70,
n. 11. A letter of Robert, the Cardinal Legate
(A.D. 1215 Augusti) confirms this prohibition:
"Non legantur libri Aristotelis de methafisica et
de naturali philosophia, nec summe de eisdem
. . ." *CUP,* I, 78, n. 20. See: Van Steenberghen,
F., *Aristote en Occident,* (Louvain, Institut Sup.
de Philos., 1946) pp. 63-86, for a recent sur-
vey of these prohibitions.

5. "Ad hec jubemus, ut magistri artium unam
lectionem de Prisciano et unum post alium ordi-
narie semper legant, et libris illis naturalibus, qui
in Concilio provinciali ex certa causa prohibiti
fuere, Parisius non utantur, quousque examinati
fuerint et ab omni errorum suspitione purgati."
Gregorius IX ad magistros et Scholares Parisien-
ses, 1231 Aprilis 13, Laterani, *CUP* I, 138, n. 79.
The three scholars appointed to study these works
are named in this letter (p. 143, n. 87) ; Guillel-
mus archdiaconus Belvacensis, Symonus de

Alteis Ambianensi, and Stephanus de Pruvino Remensi.

6. Philip the Chancellor cites the *Ethics* thirty-two times; Roland of Cremona, thirty-five times; and William of Auvergne about ten times. See: D. A. Callus, O.P., "Introduction of Aristotelian Learning to Oxford," *Proceedings of the British Academy,* XXIX, London, 1944) p. 5, note 4.

7. Van Steenberghen, *op. cit.,* pp. 122-123.

8. Cf. B.C. Kuhlmann, O.P., *Der Gesetzbegriff beim hl. Thomas von Aquin im Licht des Rechtsstudiums seiner Zeit* (Bohn, Hanstein, 1912) 185 pp. Father Kuhlmann points out (p. 103) that the famous passage in which Aquinas condemns the subordination of theology to the authority of the canon law experts ("inconsonum et derisibile, quod sacrae doctrinae professores juristarum glossulas in auctoritatem inducant vel de eis disceptent," *Contra pestiferam doct. retrahentium a relig. ingr.* c. 13) was written in controversy. However, St. Thomas was a mild man and this is a strong statement against "legalism."

9. M. Riquet, "S. Thomas d'Aquin et les 'Auctoritates' en Philosophie," *Archives de Philosophie* III (1925) pp. 261-299.

10. St. Thomas had some acquaintances with the standard technical terms of Greek philosophy but he does not give evidence of the ability to do sustained reading in Greek. In addition to some works of Aristotle, William of Moerbeke translated parts of Simplicius and Themistius for St.

Thomas. Cf. M. De Corte, "Themistius et S. Thomas d'Aquin. Contribution à l'etude des sources et de la chronologie du Commentaire de St. Thomas sur le *De Anima*," *Archives d'Histoire Doctrinale et Litteraire du Moyen Age* VII (1932) pp. 47-84.

11.   Bréhier's statement *(Histoire de la Philosophie,* Paris, 1927 I, p. 681) : "Les idées fondamentales de la morale naturelle sont empruntées par saint Thomas à Aristote," is simplistic. See the comment of M. Wittmann, *Die Ethik des hl. Thomas von Aquin* (München, 1933) pp. 372-373.

12.   On the character of this work, see: J. T. Muckle, C.S.B., "The *De Officiis Ministrorum* of St. Ambrose," *Mediaeval Studies* I (1939) pp. 63-80.

13.   For the demonstration of the historical continuity of Stoicism from Panaetius, through Cicero, to St. Ambrose, consult: Thamin, R., *Saint Ambroise et la morale chrétienne au IVe siècle* (Paris, 1895) pp. 189-217.

14.   *Summa Theologica,* I-II, qq. 8-17.

15   "La merveille qui soutient tout le reste dans cette morale inventée par S. Thomas d'Aquin, est le traité détaillé de ces actes humains dont la théorie de la personnalité des intellects garantissait l'existence métaphysique, mais dont il fallait examiner au concret les circonstances, les comportements. Il y a là, surtout questions VI à XXI de la Ia IIae, un ensemble absolument neuf sur

les conditions de l'acte libre, de ses responsabil-
ités, consentements et choix, où saint Thomas
parle le langage de ses principes métaphysiques
et où l'on trouve toutes ces notions experimen-
tées en soi-même." M. M. Gorce, *L'Essor de la
pensée au moyen âge* (Paris, Letouzey, 1933)
p. 299.

16. The texts are established by Dom O. Lottin,
Psychologie et morale aux XIIe et XIIIe siécles
(Louvain, 1942) pp. 397-398 from MS lat.
14557 Bibl. Nat. f. 204vb—205va and MS 12814
—41 (1387) Bruxelles Bibl. roy. f. 127rb—
127va. See the Greek text in: *Patrologia Graeca*
XCIV, 944-945.

17. See: Aristotle, *De Anima,* III, 11; 434a 12-22,
and *Nic. Eth.* III, 4-7; 1111b5—1114a5. Consult
also the commentary of St. Thomas, *In III Eth.
Nic.* lect. V-XI (Pirotta ed. pp. 145-171, nn. 432-
496.)

18. The Latin text printed with St. Thomas'
Commentary on the Ethics (Pirotta ed., p.374)
reads: "Propter quod, vel appetitivus intellectus
electio, vel appetitus intellectivus, et tale principium homo."
    W. D. Ross translates this sentence (*Eth. Nic.,*
VI, 2; 1139b4-5) : "Hence choice is either desid-
erative reason or ratiocinative desire, and such
an origin of action is a man." See: *Basic Works
of Aristotle* (R. McKeon ed., New York, 1941)
p. 1024.

19. Cf. Lottin, *op. cit.,* p. 240.

20. In the 13th century, the περὶ φύσεως ἀνθρώπου of Nemesius (*PG* XL, 503-818) was mistakenly attributed to Gregory of Nyssa, as may be seen in the text of St. Thomas. Despite the tendency of many histories of philosophy to regard all the early Greek Catholic writers as Platonists, the Aristotelianism of Nemesius is quite evident. This is particularly true of the treatment of appetition; see: Domanski, B., *Die Psychologie des Nemesius* (Münster, 1900) *Beiträge zur Geschichte der Philosophie des Mittelalters* III, 1, pp. 129-168. Domanski comments (p. XVI): "Wir sehen bei Nemesius gleichsam die ersten Keime der Scholastik, in deren Augen Aristoteles der Philosoph κατ᾽ εξοχήν war." Cf. Lottin, *op. cit.,* p. 421.

21. The excellent historical research of Dom Lottin shows that the pre-Thomistic theologians of the 13th century, William of Auxerre, Hugues de St. Cher, Philip the Chancellor, the authors of the Alexandrine Summa, John of La Rochelle, St. Bonaventure, St. Albert, and Gerard d'Abbeville, are all concerned with this same text of St. John Damascene. (See: Lottin, *Psych. et morale,* pp. 399-413.)

One wonders whether M. M. Gorce could have looked at any of the theological texts contemporary to St. Thomas, for he wrote: "si l'on cherche, par exemple, dans la table détaillé de l'édition critique de . . . S. Bonaventure, on voit à ces mots: *intentio, electio, consilium, consensus,* que ces cases de la valeur morale n'avait pas été explicitement traitées comme telle avant saint Thomas." *(L'Essor de la pensée au m. â.,* p. 299.)

22. "Regula autem et mensura humanorum actuum est ratio, quae est principium primum actuum humanorum." *Sum. Theol.* I-II, q. 90, a. 1, c; cf. q. 19, a. 1, c; q. 58, a. 2, c.

23. *Commentum in libros IV Sententiarum Magistri Petri Lombardi* III, dist. IX, q. l, a. l,qnla. 2 c; *In VI Eth. Nic.,* lect. VII (Pirotta pp. 398-402, nn. 1196-1216) ; *Sum. Theol.* I-II, q. 57, aa. 4, 5 c; II-II, q. 47, a. 4 c.

The following lines are typical: "The practical reason must be perfected by some habit so that it may judge rightly concerning human good in regard to singular actions. This virtue is called prudence, and its subject is the practical reason. It is perfective of all the moral virtues which are in the appetitive part, each of which gives an appetitive inclination toward some general kind of human good . . . Thus, the rightness and fulfillment of goodness in all the other virtues arise from it; hence, the Philosopher says *(Nic. Eth.* II, 6; 1107a1-5) that the mean in moral virtue is determined according to right reason." *De Virtutibus in Communi,* art. 6 c. (Actually, the *Nic. Eth., loc. cit.,* just says that the mean is determined by reason.)

24. *Sum. Theol.* I-II, 13, 1, c; cf. *De Malo,* q. 2, a. 4 c.

25. For a capable presentation of this view, see: Elter, E., S.J., "Norma honestatis ad mentem D. Thomae," *Gregorianum* VIII (1927) 337-357.

26. See, for instance: Lehu, L., O.P., *La raison régle de la moralité d'après saint Thomas* (Paris, Gabalda, 1930, 264 pp.) The important texts are conveniently gathered in this little book; its exegesis is somewhat subjective.

27. "The virtue of each and every thing consists in its being well disposed in agreement with its own nature, as has been said above. [In art. 1, St. Thomas had said: "Directe quidem virtus importat dispositionem quandam alicuius convenienter se habentis secundum modum suae naturae."] So, it must be that a vice is spoken of when a thing is disposed in a manner contrary to that which is in agreement with its nature . . . But we must consider that the nature of each thing is chiefly the form in accord with which the things gets its species. Now, man is constituted in his species by the rational soul. And so, what is against the order of reason, is properly against the nature of man as man; and what is according to reason is according to the nature of man as man. Now, the good of man is to be in accord with reason . . . Hence, human virtue, which makes man good and renders his work good, is in accord with the nature of man, when it is in agreement with reason. So also, vice is against the nature of man, insofar as it against the order of reason." *Sum. Theol.* I-II, q. 71, a. 2 c.

F. Suarez concentrated on one aspect of the doctrine of such Thomistic texts as the foregoing. In the seventh Disputation of the *Disputationes Metaphysicae,* he attempted a very thorough analysis of the concept of human nature adequately considered in all its essential relationships. Suarez pointed out that man's nature includes an ordering of the physical and sensory powers under the rational, and that it also includes real relations to God, to other men, and to infra-human things. So considered, human nature is, for Suarez, the proximate norm of morality. It is not an exaggeration to say that nearly all "Scholastic" moralists have followed Suarez on this point. Father T. J. Brosnahan, S.J., has given a good standard exposition of the Suarezian theory, in his posthumously published, *Prolegomena to Ethics,* New York, (Fordham U. Press, 1941) pp. 179-191. A fuller treatment may be found in Father V. Cathrein, *Philosophia Moralis,* pp. 79-86; and one may consult his numerous articles on the norm of morality, in *Gregorianum* and *Scholastik,* between the years 1924 and 1931.

One result of this Suarezian interpretation of human nature as the rule of morality has been the simplistic conviction (more evident in his followers than in Suarez himself) that, once this rule has been grasped, one may almost automatically distinguish good from evil acts. This has led to an unfortunate neglect of the role of prudent reasoning in the determination of the moral quality of voluntary acts. As prudence disappeared from Scholastic ethics, jurisprudence and probabilism came in. St. Thomas never intended his "order of reason" to develop into the slide rule mechanism of little reflex principles, such as, "a doubtful law does not obligate." There is no substitute for prudent reasoning.

28. Cf. Gillet, M., O.P., "Notes Explicatives," in: S. Thomas d'Aquin, *Somme Theologique,* I-II, qq. 6-21 (Paris, Desclée, 1926) pp. 431-432; and 433-434. This point is also developed in: Bourke, V.J., *Syllabus in Ethical Theory* (St. Louis U. planographed text, 1946) Ch. IV: "The Rational Order," pp. 62-82.

29. "Manifestum est autem, supposito quod mundus divina providentia regatur, ut in Primo habitum est, quod tota communitas universi gubernatur ratione divina. Et ideo ipsa ratio gubernationis rerum in Deo sicut in principe universitatis existens, legis habet rationem. Et quia divina ratio nihil concipit ex tempore, sed habet aeternum conceptum, ut dicitur *Prov.* VIII: 23, inde est quod hujusmodi legem oportet dicere aeternam." *Sum. Theol.* I-II, q. 91, a. 1, c.

A good explanation of the ordering of all things, and particularly human acts, under Divine Providence, may be found in: *Summa contra Gentiles,* III, cap. 140: "Praeterea. Ubicumque est aliquis debitus ordo . . ."

30. Cf. Peghaire, L., C.S.Sp., "Le couple augustinien 'ratio superior et ratio inferior'. L'interpretation thomiste," *Rev. des Sc. Phil. et Théol.* XXIII (1934) pp. 221-240. References to Augustine's teaching in the twelfth book, *De Trinitate,* may be found in: Bourke, V. J., *Augustine's Quest of Wisdom* (Milwaukee, Bruce, 1945) p. 215.

31. *De Veritate,* q. XV, a. 3 c.

32. *Sum. Theol.* I-II, q. 71, a. 6 c; cf. q. 21, a. l, c; q. 63, a. 2 c; q. 72, 4 c; q. 74, a. 7 c; II-II, q. 17, a. l, c: where he simply says: Humanorum autem actuum duplex est mensura, una quidem proxima et homogenea, scilicet ratio; alia autem suprema et excedens, scilicet Deus.

33. *Nic. Eth.* X, 7; 1178a1-7.

34. Clement, *Stromata,* II, 21; PG VIII, 1076.

35. Cicero is a good Stoic, when he says: "Est enim unum jus, quo devincta est hominum societas, et quod lex constituit una; quae lex est recta ratio imperandi atque prohibendi." *De Legibus,* I, xv, 42.

36. Sister Rita Marie, C.S.J., has just completed an informative dissertation, to which I am much indebted on this matter: *Right Reason in Stoicism and in the Christian Moral Tradition up to Saint Thomas* (St. Louis U. Graduate School, 1947. Typescript, 341 pp.) Thamin, *op. cit.,* has made a very thorough study of the Stoicism of Ambrose, pp. 218-235. He stresses its enduring influence in this conclusion: "Si donc nous avons du stoicisme dans le sang encore aujourd'hui, nous le devons sans doute à des relations souvent renouvelées avec les maîtres du Portique, mais nous le devons aussi à ce que, grâce aux Pères de l'Eglise, grâce à saint Ambroise, jamais le stoicisme ne disparut tout entier des consciences chrétiennes." (p. 235).

37. "Haec autem fuit opinio Stoicorum, quod virtutes essent sine passionibus animae. Quam opin-
ionem Philosophus excludit in II Eth. (c. 3),
dicens virtutes non esse impassibilitates. Potest
tamen dici quod, cum dicitur quod mitis non
patitur, intelligendum est secundum passionem
inordinatum." *Sum. Theol.* I-II, q. 59, a. 2, ad
primum.

38. St. Ambrose is an exception; his *De Officiis* follows Cicero in arranging the discussion under the
four principal virtues of the Greeks: practical
wisdom, justice, temperance and courage. In fact,
Ambrose does not use faith, hope and charity as
major topics. Cf. Thamin, *op. cit.* p. 227.

39. The name *cardinal* virtue, though found in St.
Ambrose *(Expositio in Evangeli secundum Lucam,*
V, 49; *Patrologia Latina* XV, 1734), does not
come into general use until the end of the 12th
century; nor are the theological virtues so named,
until the 13th century. See: Lottin, "La théorie des
vertus cardinales de 1230," *Mélanges Mandonnet*
(Paris, Vrin, 1930) II, pp. 233-234.

40. *Republic* IV, treats the four main virtues *in
extenso; Euthyphro,* 12, gives piety as a part of
justice.

41. St. Thomas refers, *In III Sent.,* dist. XXXIII,
q. 3, a. 1, qnla. 4, resp. (Moos ed. III, 1072)
to a book "a quodam Philosopho graeco," in which
the virtue of prudence is treated. See similar references to temperance (art. 2), fortitude (art. 3),

and justice (art. 4). The editor's note sends the reader to: Andronicus of Rhodes, περὶ παθῶν.

There is a work of this name printed in *Fragmenta Philosophorum Graecorum*, rec. G. A. Mullachius (Paris, Didot, 1879) III, pp. 570-578. It is there listed as the work of: Andronici Rhodii Philosophi Peripatetici. It is printed along with a longer treatise, *Ethicorum Nicomachorum Paraphrasis, (loc. cit.,* pp. 303-569) also attributed to Andronicus of Rhodes. Now, there is little doubt that this *Paraphrase* is spurious. Standard reference works are almost in complete agreement in attributing it to some Renaissance classicist of the 16th century, possibly Constantinus Palaeocappa. See: Pauly-Wissowa, *Real-encyclopaedie der Classischen Altertumswissenschaft* (Stuttgart, 1894) I, p. 2167; consult also Buchbergers *Lexikon f. Theol. u. Kirche,* I, p. 423; and *Ency. Brit.* (14th ed.) I, p. 916.

The same reference works *(loc. cit.* supra) also reject the attribution of the shorter treatise, περὶ παθῶν, to Andronicus of Rhodes. It is evidently a compilation and there was a tendency among 19th century scholars to credit it to the Renaissance. However, Schuchhardt, in a Darmstadt dissertation of 1883, reported finding the treatise in a Greek MS of the 10th c. In 1885, V. Apelt placed its composition in classical Roman times: "Die Schrift ist vielmehr die Compilation eines Eklektikers der römischen Kaiserzeit." (See Pauly Wissowa, I, 2167 for fuller references.)

I have found no 20th c. study of the περὶ παθῶν but it is clear that a Latin version was known,

and much used by St Thomas, in the 13th c.
Therefore the work is not a Renaissance product.
I doubt that Andronicus of Rhodes wrote either
treatise but would suggest that it was written by
another Andronicus, who knew Stoicism well (because he uses the fourfold division of the passions:
λύπη, φόβος, ἐπιθυμία, ἡδονή, in the opening
lines of his treatise), and who was a moralist.
This corroborates Apelt's suggestion that the work
dates from the period of the Roman Empire. St.
Thomas did not know the *Paraphrase of the Nic.
Eth.*, and it may be a much later work.

42. "Affectus est animi motus a recta ratione aversus
propter quandam mali aut boni suspicionem sive
exspectationem, et praeter naturam appetitu inso-
lescens: aut affectus est animi motus a recta ratione
aversus inconsiderata nulloque judicio existens
. . ." I quote the Latin version printed in the
edition of Mullach, p. 570, because St. Thomas
did not use the Greek text; however this Latin
text is not the one used by St. Thomas. His Latin
names for the four passions are : *gaudium, tristitia,
spes, timor (Sum. Theol.* I-II, 25, 4 c.), while the
Mullach text uses: *voluptas, dolor, cupiditas, metus.*
(p. 570).

43. Thus for prudence, Andronicus says: "Comites
vero ejus sunt consilii, bonitas [sic, obviously it
should be: *consiliibonitas,* i.e. eubulia], sagacitas,
providentia, ars regum, ars imperatoria, usus rerum,
scientia civilis, privatae vitae ratio, philosophia
moralis, dialectica, ars oratoria, physiologia." (p.
574).

Cf. S. Thomae, *In III Sent.,* dist. XXXIII, q. 3, a. 1, qnla. 4: "Ulterius. A quodam Philosopho Graeco attribuuntur prudentiae partes decem, scilicet eubulia, solertia, providentia, regnativa, militaris, politica, oeconomica, dialectica, rhetorica, physica." (This is at the beginning of St. Thomas' subquestion; he goes on, in his *Solutio* (Moos ed. pp. 1076-1078) to arrange these parts under the three Thomistic divisions: integral, subjective and potential parts.)

See: Andronicus (pp. 575-576) for the parts of fortitude, (p. 576) for temperance, and (pp. 576-578) for justice. Each list is studied by St. Thomas, in conjunction with similar lists from Aristotle, Cicero, Macrobius, etc., in the sequence of q. 3.

44. For example, see the handling of the parts of prudence: *Sum. Theol.* II-II, q. 48. Here, three lists are used, those of Aristotle, Andronicus and Cicero. In the more detailed treatment of the following questions, other authors are used. Sometimes Christian writers, such as St. Gregory, or St. Benedict, are cited; usually the authorities on these "parts" are the pagan moralists.

45. *Sum. Theol.* II-II, qq. 23-46.

46. The wide gap between Aristotelian friendship and Christian charity is well described by G. B. Phelan, "Justice and Friendship," *The Maritain Volume of the Thomist,* (New York, 1943) pp. 153-170.

47. Father Angelo Walz, O.P., remarks: "Però S. Tommaso non rimase un semplice discepolo o in-

terprete d'Aristotele ma, specialmente in forza d'elementi platonico-agostiniani, si mise con le sue dottrine filosofiche su un piano di sintesi superiore." *San Tommaso d'Aquino. Studi biografici sul Dottore Angelico* (Roma, 1945) pp. 199-200.

I doubt that there is any point to which this general conclusion has more apt application, than to that of St. Thomas' concept of the real end of man. It is literally true that he lifts the discussion to a plane of thought unknown to Aristotle but not entirely foreign to the spirit of Aristotelianism.

48. Thus Father W. Farrell, O.P., writes: "It is true that the contemplation of God is the highest good in this life; but it cannot be the natural last end of man, for it is supernatural . . . The natural temporal happiness of man might be described as the possession (successive, because taking place in time) of all good things in a complete life, by means of virtue, and with the aid of fortune." See his whole treatment of the natural end, in: "Person and the Common Good in a Democracy," *Proceedings American Catholic Philosophic Association* XX (1945) pp. 41-43.

49. This seems to be the view of P. Rousselot, for instance. *L'intellectualisme de saint Thomas* (Paris, 1924) pp. 173-174.

50. See the recent study: *Surnaturel. Etudes historiques,* by Father Henri de Lubac (Paris, 1946, 498 pp.) for a well-documented account of the role

played by the term, *supernaturalis,* in the history of Catholic theology.

51.   The question is answered formally: *Sum. Theol.* I-II, q. 1, a. 5, "Utrum unius hominis possint esse plures ultimi fines." St. Thomas says in reply: "Dicendum quod impossibile est quod voluntas unius hominis simul se habeat ad diversa, sicut ad ultimos fines."

52.   Two things are to be noted in the exposition of St. Thomas: (i) man's perfect happiness can only be found in the vision of the divine Essence ("Dicendum quod ultima et perfecta beatitudo non potest esse nisi in visione divinae essentiae." *Sum. Theol.* I-II, 3, 8 c.) ; (ii) this vision of God's Essence exceeds the natural powers of any creature, and so of any man ("Omnis autem cognito quae est secundum modum substantiae creatae, deficit a visione divinae essentiae, quae in infinitum excedit omnem substantiam creatam. Unde nec homo nec aliqua creatura potest consequi beatitudinem ultimam per sua naturalia." *Sum. Theol.* I-II, 5, 5 c.)

St. Thomas often speaks (see the beginning of the article just cited, for instance) of an imperfect happiness *(beatitudo imperfecta)* which is attainable in this life, if man is fortunate. He does not suggest that this is an *ultimate* end. Nor does he think, as Father P. Descoqs seems to have thought (see the references to *Le mystère de notre élévation surnaturelle,* pp. 125-133, and *Institutiones metaphysicae generalis,* pp. 551-553, and the analyses of this view, in De Lubac, *op. cit.,* pp. 439-447.) that a "natural" vision of the divine Essence, below the level of the beatific vision, is possible to man in a future life.

53. *Eudemian Ethics,* 1246b37-1248b11; and *Magna Moralia,* 1206b-1207b19. Fortunately, it is not necessary to discuss here the question of the authenticity of these treatises. They are products of the early Aristotelian school, possibly of Aristotle himself.

54. Cf. Th. Deman, O.P., "Le 'Liber de bona fortuna' dans las théologie de s. Thomas," *Revue des Sc. Philos. et Théol.* XVII (1928) pp. 38-58.

55. A. Touron, O.P., in his celebrated work, *La Vie de S. Thomas d'Aquin* (Paris, 1740) shows very sound judgment in the following conclusion on the influence of the ancient philosophers on St. Thomas: "En un mot il profite de tout ce qu'il y avoit de sagesse, et de vérité dans ces Livres, non seulement pour sapper les fondemens de l'erreur, et prémunir les domestiques de la Foi contre les vaines subtilités de ceux qui faisoient profession de la combattre; mais encore pour éclaircir les principes de la morale chrétienne . . ." (p. 397).

56. *Expositio in Symbolo Apostolorum,* c. 1; *Opuscula* ed. Mandonnet, IV, 350.

Index of Proper Names

THE AQUINAS LECTURES

Published by the Marquette University Press,
Milwaukee 3, Wisconsin